THE FOOD PARADE

Healthy Eating with the Nutritious Food Groups

A WHOLESOME BOOK ABOUT FOOD

ELICIA CASTALDI

Christy Ottaviano Books

HENRY HOLT AND COMPANY • NEW YORK

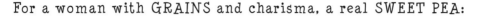

For a woman with GRAINS and charisma, a real SWEET PEA:

my mom

(CERTIFIED HEALTH NUT)

Henry Holt and Company, LLC
Publishers since 1866
175 Fifth Avenue
New York, New York 10010
mackids.com

Henry Holt® is a registered trademark of Henry Holt and Company, LLC.
Copyright © 2013 by Elicia Castaldi

Library of Congress Cataloging-in-Publication Data
Castaldi, Elicia.
The food parade : an introduction to healthy eating for kids / Elicia Castaldi. — First edition.
pages   cm
Summary: "It's time to celebrate with the five basic food groups. The mayor of Food Town introduces each
food group as they march in the town parade, from the vegetables, fruits, and legumes to the grains and fats.
Kids learn about the importance of all the food groups and how our bodies benefit from each. There is also
helpful information on portion size and exercise along with both illustrations of the Food Pyramid
and the newly introduced food plate" —Provided by publisher.
ISBN 978-0-8050-9176-2 (hardback)
[1. Diet—Fiction. 2. Food habits—Fiction. 3. Parades—Fiction.] I. Title.
PZ7.C268584Foo 2013   [E]—dc23   2013030103

Henry Holt books may be purchased for business or promotional use. For information
on bulk purchases, please contact Macmillan Corporate and Premium Sales Department
at (800) 221-7945 x5442 or by e-mail at specialmarkets@macmillan.com.

First Edition—2013
Acrylic paint, collage, and Adobe Photoshop were used to create the illustrations for this book.

Printed in China by South China Printing Co. Ltd., Dongguan City, Guangdong Province

1 3 5 7 9 10 8 6 4 2

It's mealtime!
As mayor of Food Town
I welcome you to the
food parade.

FOOD
PARADE

Dairy

Fruit

Grains

Vegetables

Protein

TOWN
PLATE
HALF FULL OF FRUITS
AND VEGETABLES

All **FIVE** major food groups join the celebration.

The food groups come together to make a balanced diet. These foods are GRAINS, VEGETABLES, FRUIT, DAIRY, and PROTEIN.

Each one is super important to our health.

Take your places, everyone,
and let the parade **begin**!

GRAINS

The GRAINS are first in line.

"Everyone loves PANCAKES!"

PANCAKE

BRAN MUFFIN

NOODLE

PITA POCKET

WHITE RICE

CRACKER

OATMEAL

GENUINE OATMEAL OATS

ENGLISH MUFFIN

MACARONI

"WHOLE GRAINS are rolling in nutrients!"

PRETZEL

ROLL

BROWN RICE

BAGEL

Bread

RAVIOLI

CROISSANT

CEREAL

BREAD

BARLEY

GRAINS have carbohydrates that give us energy to go to school and exercise.

CARBOHYDRATES are found in lots of foods.

"**WHOLE** grains are grains that are in their natural state, not processed."

BRAN

Foods high in fiber, like bran muffins, are especially helpful to our digestive systems.

If a grain is WHOLE, it's at the head of the class.

QUINOA (pronounced KEEN-wah) is an ancient Incan seed that is eaten like rice.

GENUINE OATMEAL OATS

THE GRAIN GATSBY

CARB DIGEST

VEGETABLES

The food parade is on its way as the
VEGETABLES
make a colorful appearance.

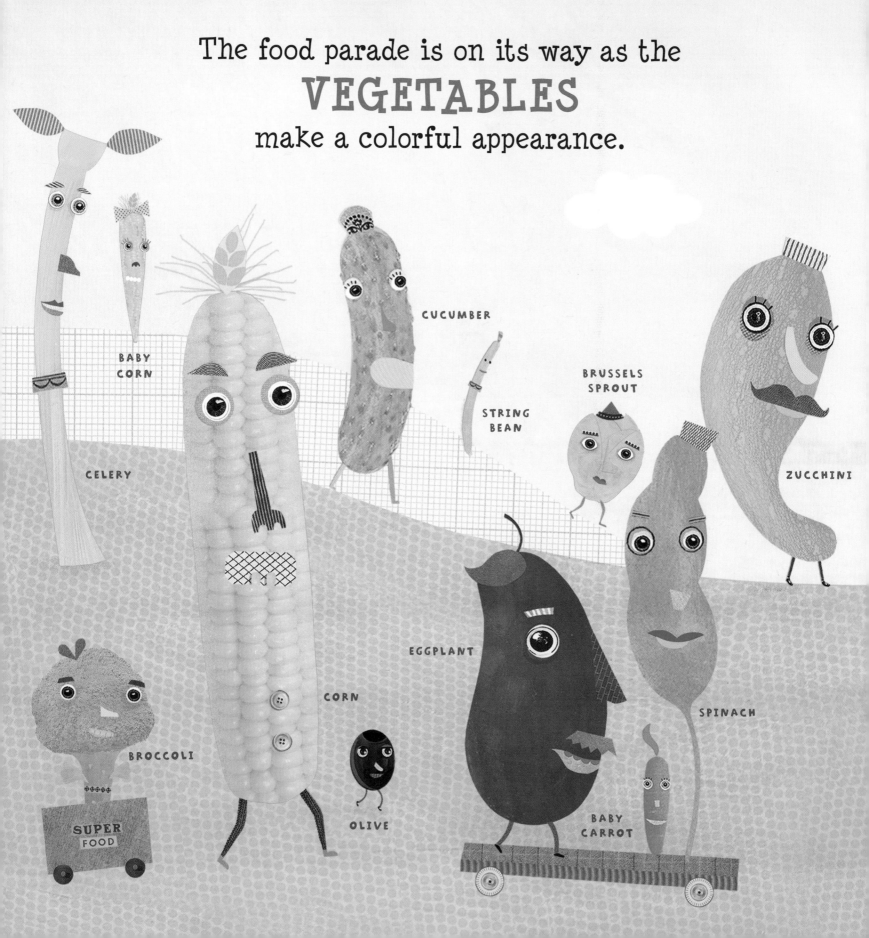

BABY
CORN

CELERY

CUCUMBER

STRING
BEAN

BRUSSELS
SPROUT

ZUCCHINI

CORN

EGGPLANT

SPINACH

BROCCOLI

SUPER
FOOD

OLIVE

BABY
CARROT

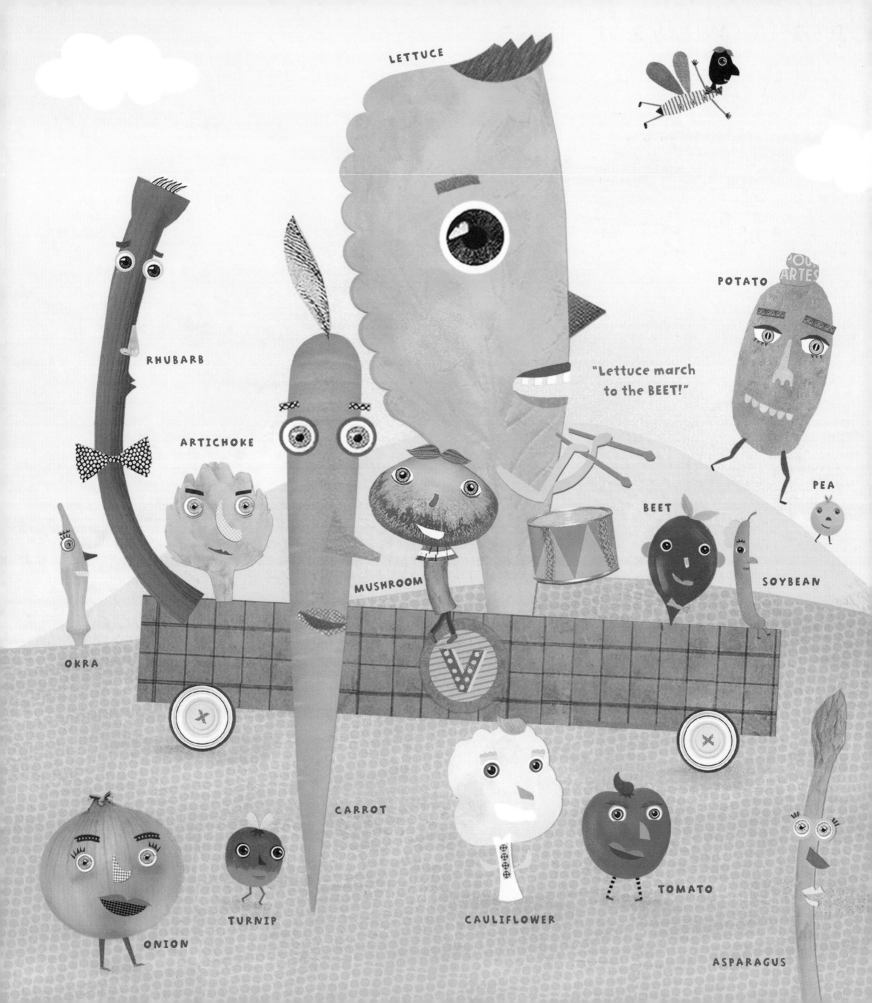

VEGETABLES get their bright colors from the many nutrients they contain.

SWEETS don't have a lot of nutrients, that's why we only eat them in small amounts.

LESS NUTRITIOUS

"Even a baby carrot has more nutrients than a cupcake."

BEAUTIFUL
E AWARDED TO
F THE LUCKY
WINNERS MUST BE

NUTRIENT SCALE

MORE NUTRITIOUS

Test your nutritional SUPER POWERS.

NUTRIENTS are the vitamins and minerals that make foods nutritious.

FRUITS

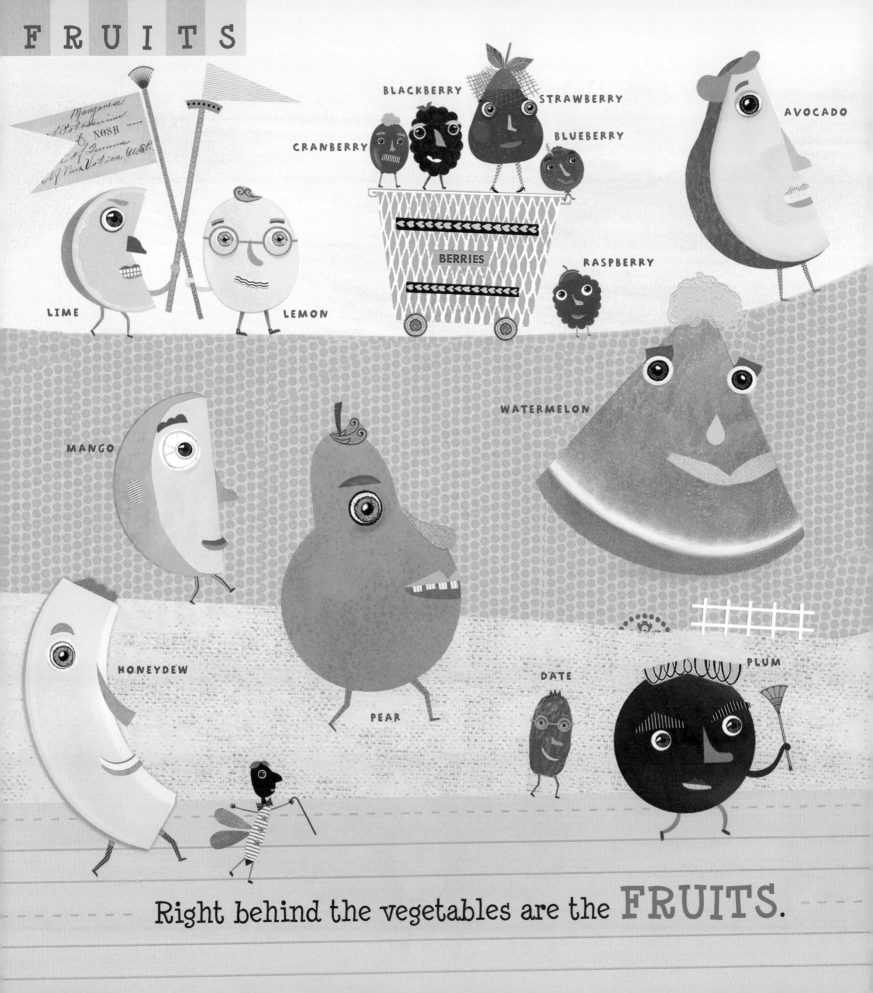

LIME

LEMON

CRANBERRY

BLACKBERRY

STRAWBERRY

BLUEBERRY

RASPBERRY

BERRIES

AVOCADO

MANGO

WATERMELON

HONEYDEW

PEAR

DATE

PLUM

Right behind the vegetables are the FRUITS.

TANGERINE

GRAPE

PEACH

ORANGE

LAKE SOUPERIOR

BANANA

CHERRY

GRAPEFRUIT

APRICOT

KIWI

APPLE

These special SWEETS are delicious AND good for us.

FRUITS are beneficial in many ways.

They contain lots of **WATER**, which hydrates our bodies so our organs work properly.

CITRUS fruits, like oranges and lemons, are natural antiseptics (GERM KILLERS).

"We're yummy and full of vitamins!"

DARK-COLORED fruits, such as berries, have antioxidants, which purify our blood and keep our skin healthy-looking.

Fruits are filled with VITAMINS, including vitamin C, which helps us get better when we're sick.

MOZZARELLA

STRING CHEESE

SKIM MILK

Skim Milk

SWISS

TO OPEN

COTTAGE CHEESE

2% MILK

GOUDA

YOGURT

CHEDDAR

Now it's time for DAIRY to MOO-ve through the parade!

Milk and cheese contain CALCIUM, which helps our bones grow and makes our teeth and hair shiny.

Yogurt contains GOOD BACTERIA,
which can soothe our tummies.

Chicken, fish, and meats contain IRON that makes our muscles strong.

Beans have **FIBER** that helps with our digestion.

"BURP! Excuse me!"

Nuts have natural **OILS** that help protect our skin.

Let's give a cheer as all the
NUTRITIOUS foods join together.

HOORAY for good foods!

"After all that activity, it's time to HYDRATE."

May all your meals be
HEALTHY!

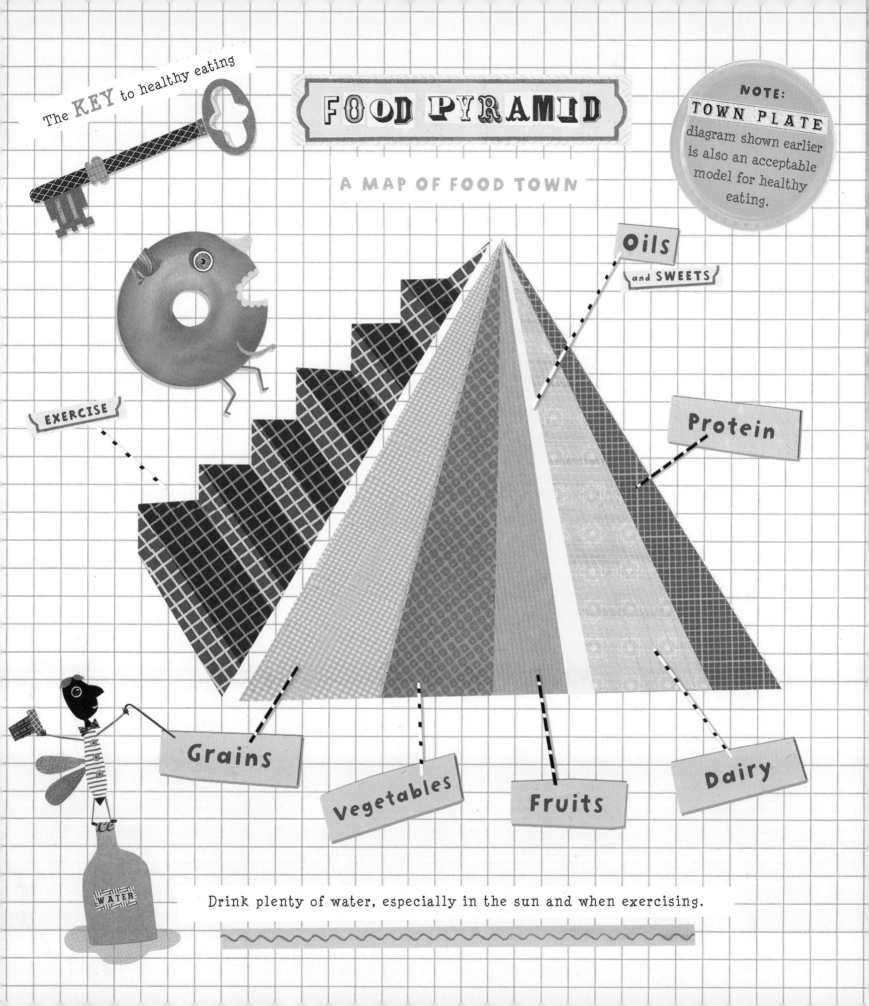

SOMETHING TO CHEW ON
A Message for Parents and Caregivers

Eating healthy foods is one of the best gifts we can give to ourselves. When we eat foods that contain lots of nutrients, it helps our bodies develop and function their best. When we eat "junk food," like French fries and candy, sometimes our stomachs have temper tantrums. This is because our bodies weren't designed to run on unhealthy food.

But before piling a truckload of parsnips on your plate, let's dish about something called portions. A portion is a measurement used to estimate how much is the right amount of food. Because adults are bigger, they need more food than children. Eating more food than our bodies need is what makes us feel full and sluggish.

Nowadays we can find muffins and bagels the size of flowerpots. Just because they come in this size doesn't make them appropriate portions. This is especially true when it comes to feeding children who have smaller caloric needs than adults. It's time for parents and caregivers to involve kids in figuring out their portion sizes. Making memorable meals instills a respect for the art of eating. Wellness is contagious!

>>>>>>>>>>>>>>>>>>>>>>>>>>>>>>>>>>>>>

Daily serving suggested for children ages 4 to 8
(One per serving in each category)

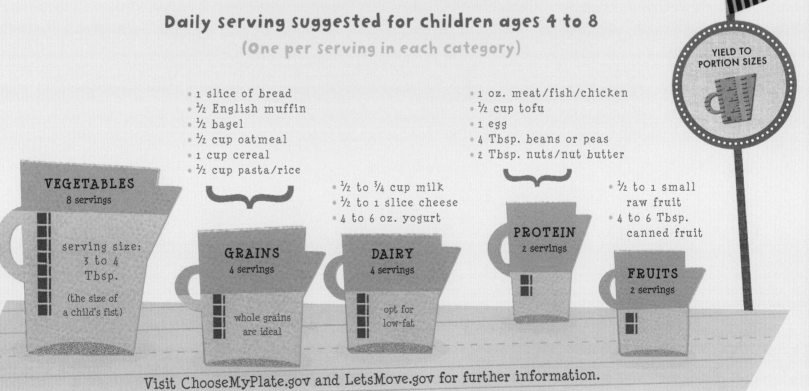

YIELD TO PORTION SIZES

- 1 slice of bread
- ½ English muffin
- ½ bagel
- ½ cup oatmeal
- 1 cup cereal
- ½ cup pasta/rice

- 1 oz. meat/fish/chicken
- ½ cup tofu
- 1 egg
- 4 Tbsp. beans or peas
- 2 Tbsp. nuts/nut butter

- ½ to ¾ cup milk
- ½ to 1 slice cheese
- 4 to 6 oz. yogurt

- ½ to 1 small raw fruit
- 4 to 6 Tbsp. canned fruit

VEGETABLES
8 servings

serving size: 3 to 4 Tbsp.

(the size of a child's fist)

GRAINS
4 servings

whole grains are ideal

DAIRY
4 servings

opt for low-fat

PROTEIN
2 servings

FRUITS
2 servings

Visit ChooseMyPlate.gov and LetsMove.gov for further information.

GLOSSARY

ANTISEPTIC. A substance that destroys microorganisms that carry disease.

BACTERIA. Microscopic organisms that are on and inside most things; some bacteria are harmful but others are good for us.

CALCIUM. An element that is in lots of foods, especially dairy items; it is essential to bone and teeth development in children.

CARBOHYDRATES. Organic compounds found in most foods, especially grains; carbohydrates provide us with energy.

FIBER. Rough plant matter that when eaten encourages our intestines to eliminate toxic waste; sometimes fiber-rich foods are called roughage.

GRAINS. Small seeds that are harvested from cereal grasses.

HYDRATE. To supply water or moisture to something; to drink water.

IRON. An essential mineral that delivers oxygen to our bloodstream.

MINERALS. Inorganic substances that help regulate body processes; potassium, iron, zinc, and sodium are examples of minerals found in food.

NUTRIENT. Chemical substances in food that provide energy, help bodily functions, and build new structures.

NUTRITION. The process of using nutrients to feed the body, helping to maintain health.

OIL. A thick liquid found in plants that are high in fat, such as olives. Eating oil and fats is necessary for our bodies to function (especially our brains), but too much of it isn't good for us.

PROTEIN. An organic component in most foods that helps us build our muscles, organs, and immune system.

VITAMINS. Beneficial organic nutrients that maintain growth and normal metabolism; the healthiest foods have lots of vitamins.

WHOLE GRAINS. Grains that contain the complete grain kernel: the germ, the bran, and the endosperm; grains that have been minimally processed.